ONLY LOVE CAN DO THAT

April Rooks

To my sweet friend
Kelli,
May you continue to
be a light in the world.
Much love,
April Rooks

A portion of the book proceeds goes to the Amped Kids Foundation providing foster children music education in Georgia.

Cover design by Susan Daniel and April Rooks
http://creativeinconline.com/

ISBN: 978-1-7044-8301-6

ACKNOWLEDGMENTS

To my beautiful family – Nathan, Preston and Cheyenne for teaching me how to love unconditionally and working together daily to be love in each other's lives.

To my mom and for all the love and support you have shown in my life. Mom: you have shown me the power of a Mother's love that has fiercely loved, protected, given selflessly and shown endless grace. Dad: you laid a foundation of faith and compassion for those in need through serving together for the least of these.

To my Grandma who is in heaven who truly imparted a legacy of love and service that inspired me to keep going in the face of my failures and pain. (Inez Allison)

To my Aunt Janet for supporting my music, each endeavor and being not only family but a mentor in my life.

To Tod Peavy and Nishala Botts for your courageous hearts and willingness to share your story and to be a light to others who are seeking a path to healing and forgiveness.

To God, the Giver of Life, for the gift of music, songwriting, creativity and the ability to touch lives in small yet miraculous ways. Thank God for letting me go through hell, make terrible decisions and go through all that I have so I could be more loving and compassionate to a world that needs understanding, compassion and more love.

CONTENTS

CALLED TO LOVE

There is nothing greater than the call to love one another. It is the highest call for all humanity. Loving others should be the ultimate goal in everything regardless of our race, religion, beliefs, culture or career path we choose.

We all need to feel loved and accepted. We long and strive for love, often doing desperate things to obtain what we consider love. We want people to love us and give us validation. It is important to understand that love is not to be confused with dependence nor is love simply an emotionally based feeling.

True love begins with loving and accepting yourself. The journey of loving ourselves begins in knowing we are intrinsically connected to our Creator. He has made us all connected within our Source, God. God is love. There is nothing that could separate any of human creation from that love. No mistake that you could possibly make would cause Him to love you any less. There is no path you take that he is not walking with you. Nothing can separate you from the love of God.

During my childhood, I never questioned I was loved. I was fortunate to have a loving mom and dad. Although my parents were divorced, my dad was active in my life. I was raised in church with morals and values. But there is also alcoholism, drug abuse, physical and verbal abuse, codependency and a lot of grudges and pain weaved into my family's story. Family holidays and birthday parties ruined by drinking and fighting. Chaos and dysfunction among family members being in and out of jail countless times. Black eyes, DUIs and not being able to talk about the issues and hurt between siblings.

I would find myself marrying into the same abuse pattern at the age of 20. Over four years of verbal abuse, aggression and living with a binge alcoholic, I had lost myself. I lost my self-worth. The abuse, abandonment, betrayal and bitterness took over my life. I began to look for validation and love in the wrong places. My heart was broken, and I felt I had absolutely nothing left. I had forgiven, but I had not completely let go and healed. I was very empty inside because I had lost the love for myself.

After nine years of living this broken cycle as a single mom, I began to truly forgive not only my ex-husband but my parents as well. The root of bitterness is a systemic and deep-reaching web of unforgiveness, pain and wounds that need healing. Like a root that is causing damage underneath the surface of the earth to other plants and foundations of homes, the root of bitterness has to be plucked up and thoroughly removed.

When we do not address wounds, we begin to turn to ego rather than to God. The hurt causes us to believe we cannot trust anyone. We may come to a place where we do not even trust God. If you have experienced this, you are not alone.

If we view our experiences from a higher perspective, we see there must be a fall to precede rising. Think of how the tide goes out and comes in. Through every shift, fall or seeming adversity, there is blessing. The blessing is in the person you are becoming through each experience. Every experience is intended for our good. In fact, it is through the darkest times and hardest moments, we are gaining skills and learning valuable lessons for our next season. You see, there is no obstacle to the mind of God. It is simply the process of learning, growing, and becoming more aligned with our Creator, who is Love. And, at each intersection, we have a choice. We have the opportunity to choose love, or we choose to live in fear. Let's look at how those choices affect our lives.

Our ego is our baser self, our instinct, and is ultimately concerned with only itself. Ego says things such as, "If I don't look out for number one, no one else will." It keeps us from trusting, loving, believing, hoping, and essentially keeps us from living our best lives.

I remember how I lay in my bed night after night covering my pillow in tears and mascara because the man I married and thought I could trust lied to me, betrayed me, and left my son and I. I wailed over the fact that I was a single mom and never saw my life looking this way. There was a deep feeling of failure because I was warned by friends and family not to marry him. I did not listen. I was angry at myself. I was angry at God and living in fear of the present and my future.

Fear robs us of our peace because we are only looking to serve ourselves or we are holding onto the bad things someone else did to hurt us. Ego whispers there is not enough for all of us and we must not give to others because we have to protect what we have. Fear is when we forget that we are a part of God's design. How can we be at peace if we have not first created internal peace within our souls?

"There is no fear in love. On the contrary, love that has achieved its goal gets rid of fear, because fear has to do with punishment; the person who keeps fearing has not been brought to maturity in regard to love" (1 John 4:18 CJB).

The opposite of fear is love. Love says there is enough for all of us; you are enough. Love says you are a part of God's purpose and plan. Love hopes. Love trusts. Mature love is not self-serving. Love gives because it is the right and good thing to do without seeking reciprocation. Choosing love frees you from the past, and choosing daily to love yourself empowers you to love others.

I am now grateful for the scars in my past. Without each of them, I would not have grown into the woman of character, integrity and love that I am today. It took the loneliness, the pain, and even my mistakes to humble me. Where I was once judgmental and legalistic in my belief system and often criticized others' mistakes and failures, I needed to truly experience the love and forgiveness of my Savior so I could have compassion.

What if the entire meaning of life is simply to grow in love?

LOVE YOURSELF

The Torah and New Covenant teach us to love God and love others as we love ourselves. Are we able to love others if we do not love ourselves? We are not able to love others completely until we love ourselves. We read that we are to be holy as God is holy (1 Peter 1:15 CJB). To be holy is to be wholly who God created you to be through loving yourself as a child of God.

Do you feel unloved, rejected and that you are not enough? Do you struggle with believing you are worthy of love and forgiveness? I remember the times I felt shame for my mistakes and could not forgive myself. I lived in self-hatred and unhappiness due to my feelings of unworthiness. When I forgave myself, I could in turn forgive those who hurt me.

It is your day. This is your time to begin the journey of forgiving yourself. Know that you are loved. You are forgiven. It is time to let go of all your past mistakes and put it into God's hands. The past is over and you do not have to live there anymore.

Maybe your husband walked out on you. Maybe you never knew your dad. Or maybe you were abused as a child by someone who should have protected you. There is pain in your story that you keep reliving every day. There is also purpose in your pain. It was not your fault. God is not punishing you. What happens to us is not our fault, but healing is our responsibility.

For almost 20 years I had the feeling that I was never enough. I found myself in a cycle of feeling unworthy of love because I believed I was never quite good enough for anyone. All my attempts to be good enough seemed futile. In 2013, I was at a worship conference in California and had this impression (that's how God speaks often to me) that said, "You don't have to be good enough because I AM enough." I understood God was letting me know I can stop trying to be enough for everyone else. He made me enough because he is enough. I am good because I am connected as one with God. I am a child of God.

We will fail, but our mistakes don't define us. We are not our past mistakes. More often than not, our mistakes can teach us and take us in a new direction that God wants for our lives, if we surrender our will and our way.

I chose to love myself, and I have to choose that every day. And when we truly believe we were created by God, who is love, we can embrace that love. Our beautiful story begins because now we can love our Creator and we can show love to others. We experience love as a verb. We see love is real and alive and a part of a larger story God is telling through us.

Healing comes in cycles and seasons, and we must love ourselves enough to listen. We heal in different ways, whether through reading books about healing and emotional health, support groups, counseling, massage, acupuncture, rest, eating well, being a part of a church, synagogue, or spiritual group, exercise, and good long cries. Allow yourself that. We are spirits having a human experience. The healing process is a spirit, body and soul journey. Walk it out. Don't rush it. Love the process. Love yourself.

BE LOVE

I certainly learned some valuable lessons about true friendship and about mature love in my twenties when I lost my job and was diagnosed with melanoma within the period of a few weeks. There were some people I thought were friends who were not there and then there were those constants in my life that supported and encouraged me. Knowing how sad it is to go through challenging times without the love of those you thought would be there has made me determined to be there for my family and friends when they need love.

Mature love is not focused on itself but is always there for others Every day we make a choice to acknowledge God and choose the higher way, love. It takes grit and determination because our ego wants to be boss. Daily, we surrender. "Your will be done" should be our daily mantra, our prayer, our meditation.

So let's be love. Because we can take our brokenness and turn it into something beautiful. We rise from the ashes. We take all the pain and channel it into purpose.

Let's be a tribe of people who are crazy enough to believe we can change the world through an extravagant, giving, selfless love. By touching one person's life in a small way we continue to heal the broken, give direction to the lost and shine a light to those living in dark places. When we show up to the hospital or the funeral home for a friend who needs our support, we are world changers. When we feed a hungry child or help an addict in recovery, we are changing the world. When we use our talents and gifts we were given to contribute to the world and mentor young children and adults, we are world changers.

I once believed that in order to change the world, I must win a Nobel Peace Prize, win a Grammy, become a millionaire entrepreneur, or be a spiritual giant like Gandhi or a genius like Einstein to really impact humanity. It is true that brilliant minds, spiritual masters and great orators do bring change. I love to see people doing random acts of kindness, but we need more intentional acts of kindness. We need to wake up every day with the intention to be world changers through our small acts of kindness done with love, above all - remembering that true success is being kind.

It is time to realize our higher selves and unite to bring out the very best in our humanity. We are all connected in our Maker, and what we do to others we do to ourselves. We cannot fight fire with fire without being burned. When we see injustice, we need not pick up our weapons but understand that love is the only way to bring hope, change and good. We overcome the evil in this world by doing good.

We need a new belief system that deepens our understanding of our interconnectedness. May we all set our life mission statement to read: To love so fiercely and freely that I will leave this world a little better than when I arrived.

As you journey through the next 21 days of meditation, take the time to ponder the action points and set your intention to act every day through love and inspiration. Reflect on how the words reverberate into your soul. Let them shape you. Speak the daily affirmations aloud. Your words are a force. Meditate daily through moments of silent reflection on the affirmation, scripture or spiritual teachings. Where our energy goes, our attention flows.

Love is the positive force that will change us and help alleviate pain, suffering, and drive out hate from our hearts. True change begins within. It is your choice, my choice. Choose love.

"Darkness cannot drive out darkness; only light can do that. Hate cannot drive out hate; only love can do that."
- Martin Luther King, Jr.[1]

PURPOSE

*The most important day of your life is when you find
the reason you are here.*

Once when I was a part of a ladies' book study, we were discussing our life purposes. Surprisingly, in this group of influential women, there were some who shared they weren't exactly sure what their purpose was. Although they had experienced success in their career paths, they didn't feel they had a calling such as other women in the group that were nurses or musicians, authors and speakers. As we shared how our purpose had transitioned through different seasons of our lives and how we used our gifts differently during those seasons, it was evident that our true gifts are compassion, love, encouragement and humility. A career path often is chosen from these inner qualities and not the other way around.

A part of our journey is becoming wholly who we are and understanding our purpose as spirit beings having a human experience. Holiness is a journey of wholeness to become in unity with God. As a music instructor and coach, I consistently have asked my students or mentees what made each of them feel alive. I have spoken with adults who are depressed or feel stuck. I asked, "What was your favorite thing to do when you were a child, and are you still actively pursuing those interests?" Many times men and women tell me how they wished they had not stopped playing piano or have always wanted to take a photography class or go back to school for another type of work. Sometimes we bury our treasure in adulthood.

It is easy to lose our sense of purpose when we bury our gifts and fail to utilize our talents or follow our passion. When we find what makes us come alive, who we are and what truly makes us whole, that is the day we truly start living. Author Steve D'Annunzio states in his book, *The Prosperity Paradigm*, "soul purpose is your unique series of talents, strengths, passions, interests, hobbies, attitudes and values that form the essence of the most magnificent version of you" (p. 38).[2] You have buried within your soul treasure that only you can reveal to the world and make it more beautiful. You are unique, a masterpiece of our Creator and have a purpose only you can fulfill.

* * *

Action Steps

What is your greatest strength?

What are your talents and gifts?

In a notepad, write three things that make you feel fulfilled and alive. Take your calendar and schedule those in the next week.

When you lie down to sleep, take a few minutes to meditate on what made you happy and fulfilled during that day.

Affirmation

I was born with a purpose that only I can fulfill. My passion is my purpose.

(There are tests for spiritual gifting available online. Also, consider the DISC test or the StrengthsFinder test.)

PEACE

Peace comes when we are whole.

Wâhat comes to mind when you think of peace? Do you wish you had more peace in your life? Maybe you think of wars ending, no more hungry children, no more divorces, and the thirst for political power would vanish? Comically, I remember as a child watching the Miss America pageants and hearing the common response by a contestant that they would like to see world peace. That is a lofty but admirable goal.

In Judaism, peace is taught as being at a place of completeness and balance within our self. Peace is an inside job. Our individual growth through prayer, meditation and creating balance in every aspect of our lives will allow us to come into a state of peace. When we learn to manage conflict in a healthy and assertive way and choose not to allow our emotions to control us in unhealthy ways, we bring more peace into our lives.

One of the elements of peace is being able to say "no" when we need to and also being able to say "yes" to what we should. How often do we unknowingly create conflict through saying yes to people when we aren't comfortable with that decision? Learning to be assertive and living in integrity helps maintain peace and balance. Sometimes a part of peace is confronting an uncomfortable situation. Letting our spirits be unresolved will make us feel very unsettled and hold us back from moving forward.

When we have found balance and completeness, we begin to learn how to create more peace in the world around us and become peacemakers.

* * *

Action Steps

What is keeping you from inner peace?

Make peace with someone you have been at odds with by a face-to-face conversation or letter.

Is your current career causing inner conflict? Who should you make peace with?

Affirmation

I am at peace. I create peace where there is conflict.

LOVE

If we want love, we must sow seeds of love.

When my son was five years old, we were at home in our apartment one afternoon, and he was playing with his matchbox cars. The intuitive mom that I am noticed something was off with him. I was a single mom working during the day and playing music many nights, so I was worried that I wasn't spending enough quality time with him. As I had sensed, I wasn't. From that point on, every day when we got home I took 30 minutes to play cars or whatever his heart's desire was to do together.

Life consists of those small daily moments of dinner together, a soft touch on the arm, a good hug or a warm smile when you walk through the door. Being in the moment with someone and giving our undivided attention can impact someone's life for the better. We see how love is a verb when our family, our friends show up when we have a flat tire, hold our hand before a surgery or listen to our hearts when we've gone through a divorce or break-up. For God is love, and through each act of love we are a part of God.

Pure love is patient, kind, forgiving and chooses to let go of how another has hurt you. Love isn't static. It is moving, bending, and willing to give and overlook the wrong done.

The most refined love of God finds the will to love the unlovable. Sometimes those who need love the most will ask for it in unloving ways. Our love overcomes fear and hate. When we act lovingly, we dispel distrust, insecurity, inadequacy and worry. When we show love, we are letting others know they are valuable and they are worthy of love. I am convinced at the end of our lives what will matter most is not how much money we have in the bank account, or what title or position we held, but how much we loved each other.

* * *

Action Steps

Find ways to show love. Here are some examples:

- ❖ Visit your parents or grandparents.
- ❖ Take a meal to a sick friend or neighbor.
- ❖ Take time to listen to a coworker who is struggling with a life situation.
- ❖ Leave love notes for your spouse, significant other, or children.

Affirmation

Today, I choose love. I choose to be love in what I say and in my actions. I pursue love at all costs.

GRATITUDE

Begin each day with gratitude.

Greet every new sun with a smile and appreciation for life. When you get out of bed each morning, take a deep breath and say, "Thank you." We truly must devote ourselves to learning the art of gratitude. That begins with small things and in small ways. We take a step and begin training our minds to look for the positive things and moments throughout our day, whispering an inner thank you for it all. We cannot have a negative mind and live a positive and happy life. The best practice is adding more positives until we eliminate the negative.

Six years ago, I met a vivacious lady, Ginny, through a business colleague. After knowing me for a short time, she sent me a handwritten note. It was a simple note to tell me how much she appreciated our new friendship. I felt significant and that my friendship mattered. As she extended her gratitude in one small gesture, the world shifted – my world shifted.

From that moment, I decided I was now a person that shows gratitude. Now, I regularly send handwritten notes expressing my gratitude and thankfulness to friends, family and those I work with. It is important to make others feel special, valued and to recognize the light that is in them.

You can never go wrong beginning your day with an attitude of gratitude. What are you grateful for today?

* * *

Action Steps

Each morning and night write one thing you are grateful for that day in a notepad or begin a gratitude journal.

Send a handwritten note to someone you would like to show appreciation to.

Affirmation

I am thankful for life today and for each moment it brings. I live in gratitude for who I am, for others knowing that they are divinely a part of me and for all things entrusted to me.

FORGIVE

Fear is the friend of unforgiveness.

There is a saying that choosing not to forgive someone is like drinking poison and expecting the other person to die. The sting of lies, betrayal and hurtful words or actions can leave a deep root of bitterness that weaves a destructive web in our lives. Although we are often justified in our anger, the outcome of choosing not to forgive only hurts ourselves. Anger and unforgiveness eat at our soul. Many people choose to stay imprisoned to what others have done to them. Robbed of happiness in their relationships, they live miserable existences of bitterness, anger and denial. Unforgiveness is a thief of joy.

If we repress things in our life or suppress our feelings, needs and boundaries, we will be *depressed*. When we choose to forgive, we free ourselves from an internal prison. When we choose to forgive, we are acting in love to ourselves and to those who have wounded us.

* * *

Action Steps

Make the choice to forgive. Write a letter, make a phone call or just speak out loud that you forgive that person for hurting you. It's important that you speak it out loud. Our words speak life and create the realities we determine. Each and every time you are reminded of how that person hurt you, right where you are, speak out loud once again, "I forgive you. I let it go. I give it to God."

If you have hurt someone, call them to apologize and ask for their forgiveness. Make things right and live at peace with people as much as possible on your part.

Affirmation

(Insert name) _____, I forgive you. I let it go. I give it to God.

SAY YES

Just say yes.

There are two types of people: those who like certainty and those who are okay with uncertainty. I will admit when I go to a restaurant I usually order the same thing. I choose to do the same activities over new ones.

When I was dating my husband, we took a trip to Florida. Going on a trip with him was a huge step in my life of learning to say yes. During this trip, we went kayaking. While I was very excited, I had never kayaked much less on a river where there are alligators. As we maneuvered the twists and turns, we ended up running into the riverbank. I started screaming because I remembered the sign about alligator nests and I didn't even know what one looked like. It was a scary moment, but the overall experience was fun and worth it.

I'm so glad I said yes to that trip and learned to say yes to all life has to offer me. Of course we must use our reasoning, but if you're allowing fear of uncertainty to hold you back from truly living life to the fullest, it is time to say "YES!"

Don't be a bystander of life watching as others explore. Dream and enjoy the journey.

Plan your dream trip and start saving today. Schedule the bike ride at The Whole Enchilada or hike the Appalachian Trail. Go on that date. Take the guitar lessons. Life has a million beautiful opportunities and adventures if we will simply say yes.

* * *

Action Steps

What are you saying no to?

What is being presented to you at this very moment as an opportunity to say yes?

Affirmation

I am open to the abundance of the Universe, God. Everything I need and desire in my life for my fulfillment is coming to me.

SPEND TIME IN NATURE

Nature is our greatest teacher.

L uther Standing Bear, an Oglala Lakota Chief, once said something powerful and timeless, "The old Lakota was wise. He knew that a man's heart away from nature becomes hard. He knew that lack of respect for growing, living things soon led to lack of respect for humans, too. So he kept his children close to nature's softening influence."[3]

Nature is our greatest teacher. Through nature, we learn seedtime and harvest. We learn the valuable lessons of seasons and cycles such as when we observe the moon and the ocean tide. We learn about leadership and also about persistence.

I remember when I was in elementary school and we were given a seed, soil and a small cup. We planted the seed, we watered it and made sure it had light to grow. Then we waited. It took time, but eventually there was a sprout. It grew and grew until there was a beautiful blooming flower.

It seems to be the new norm in our modern society to be disconnected from nature. Our technology and busy lifestyles keep us often indoors and distracted. I believe it is important for our generation to reconnect to the earth.

We must begin honoring creation and preserving our water, our plants and wildlife. As we learn that everything is connected, we also see the lessons of stewardship, patience, kindness, gentleness and perseverance.

Nature, our Mother Earth, helps balance our mind, body and soul. By walking barefoot, we actually can lower stress, decrease inflammation and improve sleep patterns, as some studies show.

Have you noticed how children always want to be outdoors? They play with rocks, sticks, and want to jump in the mud puddles! The entire earth is our playground. Let's begin to reconnect with the earth and plant a seed today.

* * *

Action Steps

Practice earthing in one of two ways: by standing barefoot on the grass or soil, or by planting a flower or vegetable. Get your hands dirty. A wonderful and easy vegetable to grow is tomatoes. You can pot them or put them into the ground. It is a great way to start if you are new to planting.

Affirmation

I love the earth, the animals, and I will honor all living things. I am connected to the earth - the sun, the water and everything around me.

SIMPLIFY

Simplicity brings balance.

D o you sometimes feel that the world is spiraling around you? You have so much swirling around inside your head that you cannot decide which item on your to-do list you should do first.

I talk with parents who have several children with sports practice, Cub Scouts, church choir, and a schedule that leaves them exhausted and wondering how they will get it all done. We volunteer for our church, PTA, civic organizations and extend ourselves so that we are stretched thin. Children are over-involved in extracurricular activities and even church groups activities that leave families constantly on the go. We live in a fast-paced, ADD society.

You do not have to do everything. You can say no. Children do not have to do everything to be happy or to become awesome human beings. It is up to us to take back our power. When we reclaim our personal power, we will have peace.

Simplicity brings balance and peace. We need to slow down. Our bodies need it. Our spirits need it. When we learn to simplify our lives, we are learning to set priorities. Hustle does not mean happy. Busy does not equal productive or quality. We begin to simplify by eliminating all but the essential.

* * *

Action Steps

Simplify - What can I eliminate or declutter to open up space in my life?

Possessions:

Time:

Commitments:

Affirmation

I am content with everything I have been given.

PERSEVERE

Keep going.

There have been more miracles in my life than I know," Tod says as he shares about his experiences in foster care from an early age and crash landing his plane in 2017. Tod's mother was injured in a motorcycle accident where she was disabled and left unable to care for her son. Later on, his dad handed him over to foster care where he would suffer from physical and sexual abuse for six years. He was made to sleep in the basement and forced to bathe from the sink. Tod was told he was nothing but a foster child and a liar. He would go to school covered in bruises and all the while hoping and persevering for better days.

One Christmas Tod was given a model car that he proudly put together. It was one of the only things that brought him joy. His foster mom broke it over and over with Tod rebuilding it each time. "She was always trying to break me," he says. "She couldn't do it."

Prior to her accident, Tod's mom made sure he was in church regularly, and he came to develop a strong relationship with God. Tod accredits his faith as a foundation in his life that gave him the strength to overcome all he went through. During those six years of abuse, Tod prayed every day. "I knew in my heart, even at that age, if I could get through this, I would be fine once I get out of here."

Tod never gave up and became a successful Disc Jockey, entrepreneur and pilot. Ten years later, Tod forgave his abusers and says he always looks for the positive in things. He has given of his time to reach out to help children in foster care and speaks at schools and churches to encourage children to persevere. "There will always be obstacles for everyone. The obstacle can define you in a positive or negative way. You are in total control of how you will handle the obstacle," Tod said.

* * *

Action Steps

What is challenging you at this moment and causing you to want to give up?

Affirmation

I am thankful that this challenge is teaching me to persevere. There are no obstacles to God. There are only lessons and opportunities to grow. I am thankful for this opportunity. All things are possible!

COMPASSION

We can change the world: one life, one meal and one song at a time.

After retiring from education, Gene Beckstein was called to start serving those in need. He placed a sign in his yard in Gainesville, Georgia inviting anyone who was hungry to come in for a meal. From that small act of love, Good News at Noon began providing free meals, a homeless shelter, and free medical and dental services to the Hall County community.

Even as Gene grew older and his health declined, he continued to serve at the shelter. Serving there alongside him were many of the individuals he dedicated his life to along with the churches, families and community that joined his call for compassion through his servant leadership.

We are called to compassion, to defend the poor and give to those who are in need. Proverbs 19:17 says, "He who is kind to the poor is lending to *Adonai*" (CJB). Our duty is to serve one another in love every day. There are so many ways to serve. You can volunteer to cook, pack meals, hand out the meals at a local food bank, or give financially. Some of my favorite memories are with my son serving food at Good News at Noon and volunteering for the Georgia Mountain Food Bank. Serving together and teaching our children to care for others through example is invaluable. There is always someone we can help, even with what little we may have. Open your heart, and compassion will lead the way.

* * *

Action Steps

Set a time to volunteer (with your family) at a local food bank or shelter.

Affirmation

If it is to be, it is up to me. I put love into action and care for those in need.

TELL YOUR STORY

The time will come when you are ready to share your story.

Today I smile. Many years I never smiled. I remember asking myself if I thought I would ever smile a true, genuine smile. I truly believed I would never smile again." Nishala, like many other women in abusive relationships, endured mental and physical abuse fearing for her life. "For eight years I was ashamed and afraid to even mention what I was going through."

Women who live in domestic violence and experience mental and emotional abuse often begin to question their self-worth and value. A diminished sense of self-worth is one of the reasons they stay in abuse. The way they see themselves is manipulated through their abuse.

As Nishala's faith grew the year prior to her leaving the relationship, she also knew her safety was at risk, yet she had the courage to walk away. "My faith alone is what carried me out of the pits of Hell. Today, I know the strength I hold. I feel strongest as I share my story of survival. Never again will I be afraid or ashamed of my story!"

Nishala has found that sharing her story with others has been the biggest part of her healing process. It inspires her to bravely speak about her scars to others who don't yet have a voice. We each have our own story to share of our brokenness, our mistakes, our joys and our bravery. When we share our story, it brings healing. Anything that is covered will not heal.

When we get a scrape or a cut, the best way for it to heal is fresh air, exposure. You have permission to own your story, to be free. Don't be ashamed of your brokenness because it can be a part of a beautiful story of redemption and hope.

* * *

Action Steps

How will you tell your story? Write your book, write a song, or speak to civic or religious groups about your experiences to help others. Start writing one paragraph or one lyric. Start with one presentation or simply by sharing your story with one friend.

Affirmation

I am ready to share my story.

MENTOR

I am who I am today because of those who believed in me and imparted a small portion of their time, wisdom and influence.

As a music teacher, the best reward has been to cultivate relationships with young people through mentoring. Helping children recognize their value and be confident in who they are is the duty of the generation before them. The Amped Kids Foundation was birthed from teaching music and being a part of serving the local CASA (Court Appointed Special Advocates) and other foster care organizations. Amped Kids is enriching the lives of foster children in Georgia by providing free music programs. Our music programs provide tremendous opportunities for children to grow their talents, learn success principles and gain mentorships that will last a lifetime.

When I think of mentors, I am reminded of Tony Robbins who is known as the number one life coach, bestselling author and entrepreneur and how he shares the power of mentorship throughout his life. When Tony was a teenager, his father left and his mother struggled with substance abuse. While in this dark place, he began reading. On this journey of self-education, he went to a Jim Rohn seminar. Later on, Tony would have the opportunity to have the American entrepreneur, author and motivational speaker, Jim Rohn as a mentor. Tony speaks of the valuable lessons that Jim taught him but also that having many influencers and mentors in life is the key to becoming the best person you can be.

Your decision to mentor a child, young adult or even another colleague is possibly the factor that could change the course of their life. Our next generation of leaders is waiting on you. As you mentor, as you show the mentee how to apply success principles to their work and home life, as you guide them in becoming people of integrity and character, you are adding immense value that the mentee will cherish forever. Pass on the knowledge and wisdom, but most of all teach them through experience. The most important of all virtues we can teach our children is the value of character and integrity.

* * *

Action Steps

Join a mentoring program for children or begin mentoring someone who could benefit from your leadership experience and skills.

Affirmation

I enjoy investing in the lives of others. What I have been given, I will freely give.

LET GO

The secret is surrender.

S top for a moment and ask yourself what is the most difficult thing in your life to let go of? After many years of struggling with depression, being angry and very frustrated, I came to see I couldn't let go of my need for certain outcomes. When things did not go as planned, or when I came to the place where my life looked extremely different than I expected, I was angry. Ego is a force that holds onto our need to be right and our desire for our own way.

My first lesson was that of surrender. I kept going through similar experiences repeatedly. Eventually, I noticed a pattern. I started questioning why I was going in circles. God was trying to teach me to surrender.

Isn't it beautiful how the autumn leaves show us the beauty of letting go? Seasons change and things do not remain the same. Learning to let go of what is no longer for us or what may be holding us back from what we need in new seasons of life is necessary for happiness.

Learning to live for today is the place of beautiful surrender. Letting go of what happened yesterday and trusting that God has a plan through it all will usher peace into our lives. Once we learn detachment, allowing things to be as they are without trying to force change, we are free from our ego. We allow ourselves to be where we are, we learn in each moment, and we allow others that same liberty.

We cannot hold on or be attached to temporary things and be happy. There is beauty in letting go. There are new seasons, new sunrises, and new paths awaiting us.

Let go of the past. Let go of worry of the future. Let go of your image of what your life should be like. Let go of needing to have your own way. Let go of people that continually hurt or abuse your heart or body. Let go of what no longer serves you.

* * *

Action Steps

What are you holding onto that you need to surrender?

Morning/Evening Meditation: Your will be done. I surrender it to you, God. I let go of my past and put it in your hands.

Affirmation

Your will be done. I let go of my will and my way. God's way works. I trust that you have a plan for my life in every season.

SERVE

Living at the highest level of life means we should serve well and serve often.

As a teenager and young adult, I struggled with depression. After a divorce at 25 and suddenly facing the reality that I was a single mom, the fear, anger and sadness hit me. The way I typically handled conflict or challenges was to withdraw and spiral into a dark place. I began to make other negative life choices that only worsened the pain and depression.

During this time, I began to volunteer more in senior living communities and non-profits. Eventually, I had this awakening: When I was focusing so much on me and all the things I didn't have, I was sad. But when I gave to others and served others, I had joy. When I shifted my focus toward who I could serve, my heart was full. Some of the happiest people I know are those who often volunteer and give to others. They do not complain about their circumstances because they aren't focused inward.

Lake Tiberius receives from the Jordan River and then releases it. However, if you look at an image of the Dead Sea, it only receives. The definition of death is something that is only capable of receiving and does not give back. Giving and receiving together is the highest level of life.

By practicing kindness and selflessness, we align with our true selves. The true authentic self asks: "How may I serve?"

* * *

Action Steps

Remember the happiest people are givers!

A few simple ways to serve:

- ❖ Visit a grandparent or go sing or lead a Bible study in a senior living community.
- ❖ Volunteer at your place of worship.
- ❖ Help with your child's school fundraiser, reading time or other school event.

Affirmation

I am a giver. Today I will look for ways to add value to the lives of others by serving through my gifts and abilities. Freely I have received. And likewise I give freely.

GROW

We are meant to grow through our experiences.

Are you alive? Well, if you are reading this, you certainly are. Do you feel alive? That is the true question we must ask ourselves. Many people are slowly withering inside, fading from the joys and fulfilling lives we were meant to live. Are you living an abundant life?

I often encounter many people who feel stuck. They are depressed, agitated, frustrated and on the edge of giving up. When we stop growing, there will be a restlessness and that feeling of not being able to move forward. When we feel this way, it is God telling us it is time for us to grow and move. Growth always means action. It is our signal to push through the resistance. It is as simple as asking God to reveal the area of resistance or why you are in a holding pattern.

We are meant to grow through our experiences. Personal growth will mean change. While change can be challenging, it is also meaningful and necessary. Depending on where we are in the journey of life, we have different needs for growth. It might be finishing a college degree, learning about relationship boundaries, navigating through the needs and issues of parenting, or spiritual growth.

I find the storyline of the movie, *Oz the Great and Powerful* inspiring. Oz is looking to be a great magician. In his search for fame and greatness, he finds himself becoming an unexpected leader in this crazy journey of stretching his belief system and at times doubting himself. But Glinda the good witch believes in him.

At the end of the film, Glinda says to Oz, "For the record, I knew you had it in you."

Oz replies, "Greatness?"

"No, something better. Goodness."

Just as the butterfly goes through stages from an egg, larvae, caterpillar, cocoon into a beautiful butterfly, we as humans all undergo transformational stages of growth if we allow it. Let's choose to grow. We weren't meant to be otherwise. Strive to grow in goodness, integrity and eternal values.

* * *

Action Steps

Some ways to get moving!

- ❖ Take a class of interest or further education at a college or technical institute.
- ❖ Read a new book about an area you would like to grow in such as boundaries, emotional health or dealing with personal struggles.
- ❖ Begin an exercise class or get a personal trainer.

Affirmation

I am growing through what I am going through today. I am focusing on ways to expand and learn daily from my experiences and others.

LIVE INTENTIONAL

*The day you get real about life is when you decide
exactly what you want.*

It is quite easy to get in a rut and find ourselves existing rather than truly living. Desperation sets in. Years pass, and we look back wondering how or why we did not do more. We question why we aren't who we thought we should be. We wonder why certain relationships are not healthy or have gone to the wayside.

Are you at the wheel of your own life? Are you running your day, or is your day running you? There is no other path to fulfillment but intentional living. Intentional living is the road less traveled.

When you were 9, what was your favorite thing to do? What about when you were 15? Do you still actively do those things on a weekly or even monthly basis? If you're a creative person, it is essential that you create. It isn't something you do. It is who you are. If you have an analytic talent for numbers or design, run with it. Throughout life, I have seen many unhappy people living a lifestyle that is contrary to who they were created to be. It might be they chose a career for income reasons or to acquire things. They realized the house, the car, all those things didn't fulfill them in their innermost soul.

When you lie down to sleep at night, stop and ask yourself what made the day awesome. Repeat that. If you are not happy where you are, then it is time to ask what you want for your life. It is never too late to choose a new path, a new career or to begin taking time to do things that bring you happiness and fulfillment.

Always live true to you and live with intention. When you live on purpose, you will find purpose and fulfillment. Who are you and what is it that you truly want in your life?

* * *

Action Steps

How to live a bit more intentionally:

- ❖ Purchase a calendar. What needs to be on the calendar? What would you like to be more intentional about? Exercise? Creative time? Hiking or being in nature? Dancing? Family time?
- ❖ Create a vision board of what you want in your life this year.
- ❖ In the evening, write your schedule for the following day. Include the time needed for the things that make you come alive. Also, schedule certain monthly or annual trips, plans or dreams that it is time to move forward and accomplish.

Affirmation

I have been given this wonderful, beautiful, audacious life, and I am bold enough to live it. I choose to live intentionally, to live with purpose on purpose.

BE COURAGEOUS

There are angels among us who teach us how to be brave in the face of fear and tragedy.

Mike came wheeling into my driveway in his powered wheelchair alongside my dog, Becka one summer afternoon. With a big smile on his face, he began to tell me how he and Becka had become friends. We chatted about the neighborhood as I had not lived here very long.

Mike proceeded to tell me about his accident. He told me he was a trucker and had an accident that left him in his condition as a quadriplegic. As he shared about his time recovering at the Shepherd Center in Atlanta, he told me how he would help the young kids who were there also. He had a gleam in his eye as he shared stories of encouraging kids that were now in his condition not to give up.

We can choose to be a victim of our circumstances, or we can choose to be courageous and overcome. Inside of each of us is a divine strength. If we ask and we search for it, we will find it is waiting on us to call it forth.

Mike is the most courageous man I have met in my time on this planet. In the next eight years that he blessed us with his presence on earth, he taught me to be strong and courageous in the face of fear. He never once saw himself as a victim. We cannot be a victim and an overcomer at the same time. We must see ourselves as an overcomer, a hero just as Mike did.

You are the hero of your own life too.

* * *

Action Steps

When you are afraid to do something, do it anyway. Take that one small step. *Move.* Choose one thing you are afraid to do and do it today.

Affirmation

I am brave and have a courageous heart. Everything in life that has happened was for me, and I am better because it happened. I am strong, and I am an overcomer.

SPEAK LIFE

We can choose to use our words to encourage, bring love and uplift others or to be a negative energy of destruction. Choose carefully.

E ach day presents a billion chances to be a positive force for good. We have this amazing power to speak life into our own lives and to bring ideas, dreams and needs into being through our positive words and affirmations. Likewise, the words we speak to our children, our spouses, our employees and friends will impact their lives either positively or negatively.

I remember seeing an illustration of someone pushing toothpaste out of the tube and then trying to push the toothpaste back into the tube. It is nearly impossible. So it is with our words. The kids at the playground who said, "Sticks and stones may break my bones but words will never hurt me" were not being honest. Words can hurt us deeply and destroy our relationships.

There was a young woman who after multiple suicide attempts shared with me that before she took the pills she could hear her mother telling her she was worthless. These words crippled her spirit and were a framework for her life.

We need more parents, coaches, pastors and mentors speaking life into children telling them they are valuable, accepted as they are and loved. As we were once children, we recognize these are the voices they will hear throughout their lives, cheering them on and reminding them of their value.

We cannot change what has been said to us, but we can certainly learn from our experiences and begin to change what we say. How will you impact the life of a child, friend or someone you work with today? We have the power of creation through the words we speak to others as well as ourselves. We need to stop and think before we speak. Let us be mindful of the power of our words and to speak life.

* * *

Action Steps

Who has been your biggest fan or cheerleader?

An easy way to start cultivating the skill of speaking life into others is finding something to compliment others on, whether it's the person's shoes, purse, or telling our kids what a great job they did cleaning their room or helping in the kitchen. Start small. What we begin to focus on expands.

Affirmation

Today I speak life into difficult situations, and I will be a cheerleader and encourager to my spouse, my children, people I work with, and strangers. I choose to speak positively to the seemingly negative things or obstacles that come my way, knowing that I have the power of creation in the words I speak.

CONNECT

In a time of uber connection through the internet and social media, we are more disconnected and depressed. It is time for a reconnection and living in community rather than individualism.

Social media has made us virtually more connected than ever before in the history of humankind. Yet studies show that we feel more depressed and lonely. Maybe with these trends of technology and fads such as Snapchat, we are learning that there is still nothing as valuable as a face-to-face conversation or a hug from a friend.

Life consists of a billion little, magical moments like holding hands with a new love, the warm feeling of being together with coffee and a long conversation with a good friend, and sometimes a simple smile from a passing stranger. It is a reminder that we belong; we matter to the world. We are connected.

When I was about eight years old, my dad and I went to a local nursing home where we sang hymns for the patients. He also gave a message from the Bible. I can still see the faces and feel the gratitude from elderly women and men that were so happy to have us there. We didn't have money or gifts to bring. All we had was our time, our presence and our talent.

I think it is time we begin a revolution towards truly connecting with one another again. Let's shift to reality. No more smartphones creating a dumb society. Let's be intentional about putting our phones away and connecting with our family and friends. Life is not a practice run or a dress rehearsal. This is it, so let's soak it all in with every bit of intensity we can muster. Be present, and you will be the gift.

* * *

Action Steps

Take a phone break!

No social media, phones or technology for 24 hours.

Amazing ways to reconnect:

- ❖ Visit with your grandparents or a senior living community.
- ❖ Set up a lunch or dinner with a friend (no phone or cameras).
- ❖ Plan a hike with a group of friends.

Affirmation

I love to connect with others because I am Divinely created for relationship. I am intentional about carving out time for those I love and choose to make them a priority.

BE STILL

Learn to relax. Learn how to love yourself by giving yourself time to rest your body and spirit.

*B*usy. That is the response from many people when I ask how they are doing. We live in a society that is simply too *busy*. We are busy with work, school, sports, friends, church and responsibilities of modern life. Many men and women, moms and dads, and children are suffering from burnout.

The beauty of life is not found in the hurry. We find our best times with our family and friends over a dinner or a long walk. Do not get so busy that you forget to stop to smell that fresh newborn baby fragrance or hug your children before school. Let's not let the hurriedness of today keep us from living life in the moment.

An important part of thriving is rest, recharge and reconnecting inwardly. It is necessary to make time to refresh our bodies and spirits. We should turn off the television and radio, shut down the computers, phones and other gadgets that keep our minds turning. Silence is where God speaks to us. Silence is our time to listen. I believe that silence is a cornerstone of life and of building character. Let us practice the art of cultivating silence.

If you are exhausted mentally, physically, or emotionally or are experiencing depression, that is your spirit and body with a huge *Stop* sign. It is time to take a breath.

* * *

Action Steps

Give your mind and body a reset.

Daily meditation will help with beginning your day and ending your day. Meditation is proven to help mental health and reduce stress and anxiety. Take 10 minutes to be quiet and repeat the words seven times, "Your will be done."

Remembering to set aside a day a week for you to completely rest is good for your spiritual self as well as your body.

Affirmation

I will breathe. I will allow my spirit and body to rest. I am a human BEing not a human doing.

SHINE

Maybe you are in a dark place because the world needs your light.

Science teaches us that darkness is the absence of light. Imagine walking into a dark room. When you light a candle, suddenly the light dispels the darkness. Within each of us is the same power to bring light into a dark room or a dark world. As Jesus once said, "You are light for the world" (Matthew 5:14 CJB).

A favorite childhood memory is the Christmas Eve candlelight service at my church. One by one we shared our light with the person next to us until all the candles were lit. We have the same ability to unite the Divine spark in another through our light if we allow it to shine and share it. Our light is not meant to remain hidden. Light is not exclusive to only certain of us. Light is within each of us from God. We are all connected.

To the encouragers, sanguines and optimists, bounce into the room and be the life of the party. To the healers, servants and compassionate hearts, love with all your being as you feed and mend bodies and souls. To the truth seekers, teachers and wise, support and lift up those who are hungry for more. To the artists, musicians, poets and creatives, the world needs you to be their voice. In the midst of darkness, bring light, color, words and beautiful melodies. Paint the world pretty.

You are the light of the world.

* * *

Action Steps

Shine your light. It's a practical application of being love and acting in kindness every day. Write in a journal what being the light of the world means to you, or if you are artistic, sketch or paint a rendering of what it means to you to choose to love others and yourself which ultimately empowers you to shine.

Affirmation

Where there is discouragement, I give hope. Where there is fear, I give love. Where there is darkness, I will bring light.

Choose life. Choose love.

ENDNOTES

[1] Martin Luther King, Jr., *Where Do We Go from Here: Chaos or Community?* (Boston, MA: Beacon Press, 1967, 2010), 62-63.

[2] Steve D'Annunzio, *The Prosperity Paradigm* (New York, NY: White Light Press, 2007), 38.

[3] Luther Standing Bear, *My People the Sioux* (Boston, MA and New York, NY: Houghton Mifflin Co., 1928).

BIBLIOGRAPHY

D'Annunzio, Steve. *The Prosperity Paradigm.* New York, NY: White Light Press, 2007.

Jordan, Jessica. *The Gainesville Times.* March 21, 2008.

King, Martin Luther, Jr. *Where Do We Go from Here: Chaos or Community?* Boston, MA: Beacon Press, 1967, 2010.

Standing Bear, Luther. *My People the Sioux.* Boston, MA and New York, NY: Houghton Mifflin Co., 1928.

Stern, David H. *Complete Jewish Bible.* Clarksville, MD: Messianic Jewish Publishers, 1998, 2016.

ABOUT THE AUTHOR

April Rooks is a singer/songwriter, worship leader and owner of April Rooks Entertainment providing live music entertainment for weddings and private events. As a vocal and piano instructor for twenty five years, April has helped children and adults enhance their talents, build self-confidence and become successful in their music endeavors.

In 2018, April founded the Amped Kids Foundation with a vision for enriching the lives of foster children in Georgia through private music instruction, band scholarships, songwriting clinics and other music programs.

April has been married to Nathan for five years and is a mom of two children. She is a community leader, served on the board of the John Jarrard Foundation, North Georgia Senior Resources and founder of Richlife Women. She resides in Cleveland, Georgia.

Made in the USA
Lexington, KY
02 December 2019

57975938R00036